.

Virago

A Poetic Manifesto

- Fleassy Malay -

This book is dedicated to the women who's
shoulders we stand upon, the women who
have fought, suffered, and been lost.
Thank you.

It is also dedicated to my daughter, Kaia, and
the generations of women still to come. May
our steps carve a better path for you.

Poetry, text and graphic design by Fleassy Malay
www.FleassyMalay.com
Illustration by Broken Isn't Bad
www.BrokenIsntBad.com

Contents

Meniscus - 90

Howling To The Wind - 124

And So It Is... - 146

Virago: A Poetic Manifesto

I love words. It's good to note that I have not studied linguistics or literature and I'm sure many academics would cringe at my use of language. However, it doesn't change the fact that I love words. I love what they mean, and what they don't mean. I love understanding the profound effect a single word can have on a person, and on a culture at large. How combining certain words can break hearts and build revolutions. When used correctly, words can be our strongest weapon and our deepest healer.

I often find myself searching for the etymology (root meaning) of a word, exploring and redefining words which I feel no longer hold integrity or a meaning that serve me as their user.

The word Virago is Latin, and in its original form it was the name for a warrior woman. In modern tongue however, it is used to describe a woman as being overbearing, violent, bad-tempered and aggressive.

A perfect example of how in the English language, words once used to revere women are often now used as a derogatory slur. A slur designed to reduce our strength into unnecessary and inconvenient outbursts of uncontrollable, unconscious and heartless emotions.

However, even in its original form, the word Virago was not a pure dedication to the immense power and beauty of women. Virago was used to describe women who showed strength by being, in many ways, man-like. They were revered (and also often criticised) for their audacity to transcend gender roles and expectations so shamelessly.

The word Virago came to me late in the process of putting this book together. Originally, this book was going to be called, Static in The Mist. How beautiful, ungraspable; how poetic... So very suitable for a book of poetry.

So why did I choose Virago?

Because there is power in words, they can light or destroy, and currently we are are not using words to light women up, we are using them to rip them down.
Because the definition of a "Virago" as a woman who is strong because she is like a man, or, as a woman who is an annoyance because she dares to take up space and express emotions, does not sit well with me.
Because I believe change begins within.

And more so, because the sentiment doesn't rest in just this word. This insinuation that woman is less than man is echoed over and over throughout "his"tory.

The Book of Genesis says "She shall be called Woman because she was taken out of man". In Greece, Aristotle echoed it once again, "The female is female by virtue of a certain lack of qualities."

This sentiment is so deeply entrenched that there is an entitlement over a womans body, her mind, her worth. All over the world women are raped, murdered, mutilated, sold, caholed and disrespected, purely because they are seen as "less than".

In 2017 the hashtag "#metoo" (originally founded in 2006 by American activist Tarana Burke) went viral, with women all over the world revealing (and reliving) their experience of sexual violence. It was a huge time for women, not only because many untold stories surfaced, but because finally, it seemed people were listening. However, the issue of the disregard of a woman's voice and worth did not end with #metoo. This was merely a poignant (and empowering) footnote in herstory.

Women are still destroyed daily because of an intergenerational lie that has been fed to us all for thousands of years.

So often, in my poetry, women have come to me as warriors, witches, whores, mothers, lovers and daughters.

In my writing I have explored my strength through these archetypes and through my vulnerability, my pain, my grief, my sexuality, my joy, my anger and so much more.

In seven years of running Mother Tongue (the women's Spoken Word event I run monthly in Melbourne, Australia) I have never seen a woman get on that stage who wasn't a warrior, who wasn't a witch, a whore, a mother, lover, daughter and so much more. Those archetypes exist within all of us.

I have seen and felt the debilitating and traumatic effects of having our emotions, experiences and opinions reduced to the "wildness of a womans landscape"...and in 7 years of seeing thousands of women speak on that stage I can tell you, our strength does not come from how "man-like" we are. It comes from how willing we are to stand in our truth. Our willingness to face all the facets of our being; our fears, our challenges, our self-worth, our sexuality, our power, our presence. All of it. Every facet of our experience.

We are warriors in the very act of existing, and we battle every day against our own demons and those put upon us by a society determined to keep us small, nice, quiet, compliant, sexy (but not too sexy), intelligent (but not too intelligent). A scoiety determined to keep us consumable, palatable, easy to digest. Because when we diverge from these boxes we are labelled as a witch, bitch, whore, slut, frigid, angry-feminist...Virago.

I need to note, this is not a gender specific blame, it is not the fault of men. It is all of us, regardless of gender identity. It is ingrained in society, in systems and deeply ingrained in language. It has become internalised, we do it to ourselves,

to each other. Women cutting women down. Women competing and comparing. I do it too. I do it every day.

But I am committed to change.

I have titled this book, Virago, because it is my poetic manifesto of what it is to be a "warrior woman". Every chapter is another facet of my womanness, my warrior nature; every poem a battle cry.

Let this become the new definition of Virago; "A woman whose strength is evident in her courage to be herself".

So, please read these poems, be hurt by them, be inspired by them, be aroused, angered, and enamoured by them.

And know that whatever you see of yourself in these words, whatever gender you identify as, it is merely a reflection of your own strength and willingness to grow.

So thank you.

Fleassy Malay

Hiraeth
-The Longing -

Hiraeth is a Welsh word which encompasses the deep,
insatiable longing for a home which no longer exists.

This feels like a scary place to begin my manifesto, for the
first chapter to be in the depths of longing.

But it is here, in my longing, that I find my poetry is
the ripest. Longing drives me forward, the bitter-sweet,
insatiable hunger to belong.

I stumble through life with the lens of longing, in some
ways don't we all. We are born, the first wound, ripped from
the mother's womb; and spend our lives searching for that
oneness, that belonging, once again.

Perhaps Ram Das was right, perhaps we are all just walking
each other home.

*"Longing is not conscious wanting; it's an
involuntary yearning for wholeness"
| Brene Brown - Rising Strong |*

Hiraeth

I asked Google for directions
"Current location, Melbourne; Destination, England"

The page loaded, my bloodline laid out on the screen in front of
me in towns and cities threaded together with the veins of tarmac
and lights.

"Can't find a way there" was the map's reply.
"Funny", I thought, "that pretty much sums it up for me too."

That's when you know you've migrated you see,
"Home" is no longer a destination but an origin.

So we grit our teeth on foreign land,
find familiarity in the fact that everything will always be exotic
and at least that's a constant, right?

Family becomes a concept, one you can weave people in and out
of to feel safe.
We must do that, otherwise family becomes a word which is
defined by memories, and memories are, by nature, infused with
sadness...and those two words must desperately be kept separate;
"family" and "sadness".

So, we redefine our language, and we redefine ourselves.
We start new families;
ones without roots.
Ones that rip up in storms.
But we keep planting them back down, over and over again,

even if they no longer make us feel safe.
Because, if we don't have family here, if family belongs back home, then family too is no longer a destination we can return to...only an origin we came from.

Days begin to merge and we try to pretend that now is all that matters.
We wake, cook breakfast, go to work, feed the children, listen to the sounds of kookaburras, and smile.

Until autumn comes,
and the umber of oak leaves drop into the dark corners of our hearts.

Because we too are deciduous and little deaths must come often for us to survive.

Winters are hardest.
because we know
"Home" is a blooming flower,
"Home" is a summer's breeze,
"Home" is wild blossoms on the downs.
And worse than that,
We are winter.
Out of sync with our own cycles,
we are the bare branches of an oak in a vibrant Forest of green gums.
We are walking in the bloody footprints
of cultural greed
on land we did not deserve
on land we took
but we didn't take
but we are still taking.

Yet... We are on a pilgrimage, daily
to return to a place that is no longer ours,
to place that exists in the past,
to a place which is no longer ours.

Home.

Daddy

You
told me you
are the only man
I can ever really trust.
As usual, I hate to agree with you.
But unfortunately, this time,
I am afraid you may be right.

You
caught me as painfully I burst through.
Gave me my first breath.
No other man has unwrapped
from around my neck
only tied
or tried knot to.

You
carried me as painfully your heart broke.
As I shuddered in your arms,
eyes rolled back,
my body convulsing for no seeming reason.
Three days
you waited.
No other man has held my hand
when I did not respond for so long.

It is only now, as I stare
into the eyes of my own daughter
that I understand what that really meant.

You
challenge my strength with words.
Even the thought of saying
the extent of what I feel
leaves my airways choking,
chest tight,
eyes unable to keep it back.
So I don't.
Don't say it.
Not often.
Not often enough.

You
showed me how to bait a hook,
cast a line,
reminded me how many more fish there actually are,
and how big the ocean really is.

It's big daddy.

It's really big.

You
gave me space.
Gave me time.
Gave me your concern

and at times
a good solid piece of your mind.

You
will never understand

what you mean to me.
Never understand
what happens beneath my skin
and in the tiny crevices of my lungs,
when you speak of death.
of your own death.

You
will never know
the hidden tears,
the silent aching,
the gut churning feeling
of a little girl
who loves her daddy
so much
it physically hurts.

You
will never know.
Because I
will never find the words
to tell you.
I have tried
and failed
too many times.

The Girl I Was Too Shy To Be Gay To

When you are caught up
in the words
of a woman
who is published

who was once a girl
in a playground
who was too cool,
too stoned,
too unreachable,
to touch.
So, you hid in the shadows
of your overly eccentric alias
and watched from afar,
with crushing heart,
the girl you were too shy
to be gay to.

Now her words are like echoes.
The printed poetry points fingers
to your own heart
and suddenly she is you,
and she is reachable,
and real.

But she's not.
Because she is thousands of miles away,
published.
Too famous,
too known,

too unreachable,
to touch.
So you hide in the shaddows
of your overly eccentric alias
and read from afar
the words of the woman
you were too shy
to be gay to.

Waterloo Whispers

I

Nothing will ever swallow me
quite like the lick
of her gritty mouth.

She chewed me up
swallowed my teenage years
with an air of gritty pride.

Her guts became my temple,
where partly digested prayers
uttered their way through her streets,
hoping to find God
round every corner.

She embedded herself
in the tangles of my hair
and crevices of my fingerprints,
so every poem I now write
becomes a Waterloo whisper
of home.

II

I have delved into the guts
of the hungry streets of Moscow
wandered the watery veins of Venice
and caressed the coast lines
edging Melbourne town.

I touched the silken thighs of Tokyo,
watched her open, breathless to me;
writhed nameless under the smokey grip of Beijing
and slept amongst the tangled hair
of the wild Vancouver nights.

But nothing will ever taste
like the drunken kiss
of Camden town
or the sullen sigh
of a lonely Waterloo sunset.

and nothing will ever swallow me
quite like the lick
of her gritty mouth.

Virago
- The Fire -

There is beauty in a woman wild, in a woman raw, in a woman centred, and in a woman who refuses to be silent in the face of adversity.

It is not just the women who have ridden into war, suffragettes force fed in jail; it is not just women who were locked up for hysteria, or had their genitals sliced, or stood in court and named names, who are on the frontline.

It is every woman.

The frontline is our bed, public transport, our workplaces. The frontline is every magazine cover, every conversation with our child, every man leaning over in a cafe to comment on how we should or shouldn't be.

The frontline is in our minds.

This chapter is for every woman who is learning how to truly say "No".

"*A wise woman wishes to be no one's enemy;
a wise woman refuses to be anyone's victim.*"
– *Maya Angelou*

Woman-Child

A woman walked past me today
and I was captivated by her beauty
in a very specific way.
Her ruby hair tied in bunches,
her fresh face alive with life,
tattoos down her arms,
and a piercing on her filtrum
highliting the curve
of her cupid's bow.

This is not the first time this has happened.
that a woman like this stops my heart,
makes time speed up,
and captivates me in a very specific way.

Not in the way one might think.
Not with a sexual desire in my soul, though that too happens with
other women.
But not her.

You see,
when she walked past me
I saw
You.

You,
when life has taken you
out of my nest.
When your wings have spread.
Your ruby hair

a fire in the grey streets
of this world.
A symbol
that you will not take
its bullshit.
That you are here
to transform.
That you are beyond
its predefined confines.
That you will not fit
into its boxes.
That you love
like a fire,
consuming mass
in passion and focus.
That you can warm
and warn,
light
and destroy.

Girl.
Woman-child.
When women like her walk past me
their bodies fully formed,
their youth vibrant,
yet mature,
going about their day
oblivious to the effect they have
on my heart,
it stops me in my tracks.

It reminds me you will not be this small
forever,

yet you will always be
this precious to me.

That somewhere
there is a mother
sat wondering
where her little girl is right this minute.
Wondering
if her heart is happy.
Wondering
if she did it right,
if she gave her the tools she needed
to hold a sacred space
around her body
around her heart
around her mind,
if she still remembers how worthy she is
when she is out there
alone.

It reminds me
that the laughter we share,
the spark in your eyes
that lights my soul
will not always be focused
on our love.

That one day
you too will walk these streets
alone.
Head high,
filled with the drives
of a woman

like me.

This is why I call you
Woman-Child.
This is why I know
you are not mine.
This is why I love you
with all my heart,
protect you
with all my ferocity,
and hold you
with all the understanding
I can muster.

Because one day
you'll be out here too.
Walking past someone else's mother
sitting in a cafe
reminding her
of who her little girl
might become.
Making her heart stop
with your incredible
beauty.

Warriors

Sometimes a battle cry
sounds more like a battle weep
because a warrior has been slain
without her even knowing
she was a warrior in the first place.

What girl knows that?
Between the braiding of hair
and unpacking of the patriarchy,
what girl knows that her very existence
is a battle cry
in a hollow landspace
of untold truths and unwhispered secrets?

What girl realises
that she is more than emotions and expectations.
That the very act of her opening her voice,
speaking her needs,
is the raising of a sword
in a battle we did not sign up for,
in a fight we did not want,
in a role we have been told to play
for centuries?

What girl wakes up
knowing she is a warrior?
That every full-bodied breath is an act of defiance,
an act of reclaiming a body
that was stolen before she was even born?

Because it is only in these moments
when we are silenced
by the unimaginable grief
of having yet another limb ripped away
from the body our being,
when the dust is settling
on the grave of another fallen woman
who was reminded of her place
in a society which insists we are equal;
Only in these moments
is it undeniably clear

that we are warriors;

and our very existence
is a battle cry
in a hollow landscape
of untold truths and unwhispered secrets
and we can not afford
to be silent
any longer.

Even if today
all we can do
is weep.

How Many Will It Take?

How many of us
will it take?

How many of us
must revel in our own beauty
bask in our own light,
walk with our head high,
lay claim to our own bodies,
before you see
it is not yours to take?

How many of us must carry
the names you throw
with a mutated pride?
Slut. Bitch. Whore. Tease.
Shifting definitions for the sake of our safety.
Manipulating linguistics for the sake of our mental health.

How many of us
must bare our own teeth
like we do our wounds?
Must parade our scars
to make a point?
Must rip open our own healing

for your understanding?

Must use hash tags and carry pepper spray?
Must crawl our way out of victimhood?

Must rewrite our own stories
over and over again?
Before we can know for certain
you get it.

Before we know for certain
you hear it.

Before we know for certain
we can
move
on.

Leash

Alright.
I can see
you are completely in control.
You have your dog
on a leash.
You have your child
on a leash.
You have your partner
on a leash.
Who am I to believe
you have issues
with the size
of your

self worth.

But it gets worse.
as your dog
becomes more docile,
your child
begins to tug.
Your partner
begins to look elsewhere
for something
they can
love.

To food.
To shoes.

To sports and news.
To anything to fill
the void of truth.

So you grip a little tighter
to every single leash,
and you pull them all in closer
so none of you can breathe.
Your dog is looking compliant,
like all good house dogs should.
Your child is learning slowly
to be loved we must be "Good",
and your partner
well, they're still there.
Though your eyes now rarely meet,
and they've taken to decorating
their ever shortening leash.

So yes, you're in control.
It is pretty clear to me
you've got it all in an order
one that's serving all your needs.

But when the dog is dead
and your child rips off the chain
and your partner's finally realised
they deserve their own life again

When all you are
surrounded with
is leashes
hanging loose.

When your control is still tightening
into and ever constricting noose.

Right then, when all has gone,
and you are inexplicably alone;
may you realise right then
the true impact
of your
control.

Big

"What will you do
when you make it big?"
they asked her

"Spend my days
looking for somewhere
I am safe enough
to be small"

She softly
replied.

Witches

In the past they burned us
because they thought we were Witches;
just because we knew what to do with herbs
outside of the kitchen.
Because we knew how to dance,
how to seduce,
how to pray.
Because we moved with the cycles of the moon.

In the past they burned us
alive,
because they knew
that we
are Witches.

So now, we cast spells with our mouths,
pieces of our hearts spill out.
It is incredible;
the power of a woman
who is not afraid to say
"No".

No, we won't sit any longer
while you ponder on our rights.

On our rights to give or not give life.
On our rights to make another woman our wife.
On our rights to be safe,
to be paid an equal wage,
to have a voice

(You know,
in a place where we might actually make a change.)

It is incredible;
the amount of ways they have slayed
just to keep us small.
If they could have
they probably would have burned us all.
But, they couldn't with fire,
so they did it with words;
laid down laws to determine the amount of our worth.
Kept up in contracts.
Separated our circles.
Erased us from pages,
and made labour saving devices
our saviours.

It is incredible;
how quickly knowledge can fade.
How much effort was invested
to lead us astray.
But we will not come quietly.

Well,
That is another thing they have tried to take away;
our rights to exclaim ourselves ecstatically.
Uh uh
We will not cum quietly.

We will open our mouths,
let our spells spill out,
cast poetic prayers into the the night

so every woman can hear the howl of her sister's delight;
reminding her that her voice deserves to be heard.

Let her jaw drop.
Let her shame stop.
Let her body scream
under the self-pleasure of what it means
to be a woman who can speak freely.

You see words carry meaning,
and they have fooled us for so long into believing
that "No" means "Yes".
(So much so that I am almost impressed.)
Except,
I have finally discovered that they are right,
so I have claimed back that "No" as mine.
Because every "No" I throw
against their forces,
is another "yes" I retain
for my own self worth;
It is a spell I cast
for my own protection.

It is incredible;
the power of a woman
who is not afraid to say
"No".

And this old witch?
Well, I am done with broomsticks
and "know your place!"

This witch knows that some knowledge just won't fade.

That every woman is my sister,
that through the hubble and the bubble,
and the toil and the trouble,
we grow stronger
when we cast our spells together.

That we entered the fire,
now we rise from the ashes;
and we are holding our candles,
and lighting our matches,
so that the night becomes lighter
and our voices can grow,
because we have remembered
we are Witches
and we have learned
to say
"No".

Hard Work

When you tell me
that our conversations,
that our depth,
that our unpacking,
is labour;
that my emotional responses
are unnecessary.
When you say,
"I love you"
to placate, to silence, to distract,
to move on without having to...

I'll be honest,
I want to walk away.
No... I want to explain.
No... I want to walk away.
Because I think, why do I need
to be the one to continually explain to men
why avoiding discomfort
doesn't work?
Why I have no space for
superficial,
for nice,
for candyfloss love.
Why I call it the moment I see it.
Why I am not afraid of work.
Why I keep my hard basket empty.
Why, to me, love only looks real
when it is prepared to lean into discomfort

without calling that a compromise.
It is not a compromise,
it is a requirement.
Discomfort is a requirement of love.

So I want to walk away
because I've explained this gently
a million times,
and still there are times I think you see me with subtitles
written in the language of rose-tinted misogyny,
penned by the patriarchy.
I am reduced to a badly transcribed script
that has been uttered by a million men's mouths
throughout history.
"She's hard work".

I am hard work.
You are right.

But I never pretended to be anything less,
and you boarded this boat knowing full well
it would demand work,
and if you wanted an easy sail,
where you could skirt around truth,
and be met with resigned blind compliance,
you're on the wrong ship.
You know that,
I know you know that.
We've had this discussion before.

I pack up my depth.
Fold it neatly between my ribs,
origami myself back

into a consumable package;
into politisms,
and gratifying nods and smiles.
Into unimposing,
into unthreatening,
into pastel.

And you wonder where I have gone.

And you reach out for me;
question why I am holding back from you,
tell me there is distance and there is a void.

But you see,
you don't get my depths
without hard work.
You don't get my core
without being prepared to dig into your self.
You don't get to call me labour
with distaste, frustration, in your mouth;
reduce me to
unnecessary hard work,
you don't get to do that
and still get an entitlement to my depths.

I love you
and
I am fucking hard work,
and I'm proud of both of those things.

Tall Poppy

She was 14.
Born with dreams of stardom,
she'd already mastered the art of slalom
to dodge those
bullets thrown
by the harsh tongues
of adolescence.

Her spirit pearlescent.
Mind sharp,
with a curious heart,
she was the perfect target
for it.

She danced.
Spent her days entranced
with the flickering
of unreachable stars.

They called her Poppy.
Spent their days trying to cut her down.
Eventually they didn't miss,
they hit.
She split down the centre,
caught in the rift between
reality and dreams,
she fell.
Hit the ground.

No longer she danced.

Spent her days entranced
with visions of soaring high
and studying grass.
She walked smoke paved paths.

They called her Poppy
so she would fall on her ass.

But her roots were deep,
So she took to the streets
where her wit could save her from defeat.

Arm stretched,
her thumb took chart the path.
Her backpack carried heavy maps
that carved their marks upon her heart,
she touched stars.

Fallen ones, just like her.

Where needles and smoke rings had become the cure.
All stretched on cardboard beds.
All lost and found in the heart and the head.
All called Poppy,
Just like her.

Each one cut before their prime,
symptoms of a society which just isn't quite right.
Since when did it become such a crime to shine?

Poppy stared into the eyes of fallen flowers,
all doped up on reasons to escape
and realised her fate

was never headed this way.
Her demise had not begun,
her rise was on its way.
She followed with her eyes,
as the sun continued every day.

You see Poppy was not her name.
She was born a different seed.
But Poppy she became
when names get thrown by fear and greed.

Yes.
She was tall.
Yes.
She was bright.

Others, afraid, tried to smother her light.

But her heart was not blood red,
it was golden (like the sun)
and she followed its movements
from the moment it rose until it was done.

She left the streets with a knowing
that every fallen flower is a curse,
that this world will become infertile
if it keeps crushing all its girls.
She let her back stand up straight,
let her petals unfurl.
She would claim back her own name
and inspire all the world.

You see

she is not a Poppy.
She never has been.
She is a Sunflower growing
and she is full of ripening seeds.

The thing about a Sunflower
that's so special, you see,
is it is impossible to pass one by
without taking a moment to dream...

"If I had a garden"
or
"When I get back home",
"maybe I'll plant Sunflowers
just so I can watch them grow."

So, she lives like this,
leaving in her path
a trail of scattered sunflower seeds
and a field of blooming hearts.
Each turning to each other
to see how bright they can become.
Each rising with each other,
each made of earth and sun.

The truth of this story is
that every single one of us in this room
whether we are a Poppy or a Sunflower
we all deserve the right
to bloom.

Queen

Woman
No matter how low
They bow your head
That crown
Will never
Fall.

Lions

Don't tell me you love
her ferocity,
her fire,
her strength;
Unless, you can stare down the barrel
of her gun
when she inevitably points it in your direction.
Unless, you can sit in the heat
of her flames
when she calls you to burn.
Unless, you can stare back into her eyes
when she is wild and raw
and still call it strength
not weakness.

When you realise our rage
is not here for your entertainment;
is not here to make you feel better
about yourself
purely because it is aimed at another man.
When you realise our rage,
when aimed at him,
is always aimed at you;
is always aimed ourselves;
is always aimed at a society which
puts us in an arena.
Force feeds us
to the lions.
Makes us consumable.

Makes us flesh, and meat
with the inconvenient substance
and burden of bones.
Force feeds you
lies.
Force feeds you
shame.
Forces you
into becoming
lions.

As if this
is what
"pride" means.

When you can look down the barrel of her gun,
stand in her fire,
look back into her eyes when she is wild,
and raw,
and say:

"Yes. I am a lion, and I see you as meat.
But I will no longer consume what is not mine.
I will no longer hunt what is equal to myself.
I will no longer run from the responsibility of courage,
hide from the damage of my pride.
No longer stand aside.
No longer excuse its actions.
My brothers are broken,
I am broken too.

We shall always be lions,

but we shall not call ourselves a Pride
until we have something
to be truly proud of."

Then.
Then you can tell us
about the beauty of our ferocity.
Then you can tell us
about how our fires shine so bright
as they transform.
Then you can tell us
you adore our strength;
as you walk beside us
heads high.
Our paws landing to the sound
of crumbled walls
and viewing boxes.
The scattered bones of a broken society
becoming dust beneath our feet.

The arena nothing more
than a memory now,
and a reason for us all to remember
what it really means
to have
Pride.

Eyes, & Fire, & Wine

- The Darkness -

The void can seem so glamorous on the page; so poetic, so full of bitter-sweet catharsis.

Art gives us a unique gift to peer into the depths of it without having to brunt the weight of its blow.

But at some point, we must all stand on the precipice of comfort and face our darkness head-on.

And it will be excruciating.
And it will be the only way forward.

If there was one characteristic that represented what it means to me to be a warrior woman, it is this:
The willingness and courage to walk into the mouth of our darkness, to writhe and scream, disintegrate in its belly.
Then, when we are one with the darkness, to lift our heads, lean in, and rise.

"In order to rise from its own ashes
A phoenix first must burn."

| *Octavia Butler, Parable of the Talents* |

Disintegrating

How wise for the caterpillar
to cocoon itself
before this ritual.
For the rest of us
must trudge onwards,
disintegrating as we go.
Transforming under the watchful gaze
of all these elements.
Of eyes, and fire, and wine.
Howling into the darkness of our souls
whilst holding face
and looking good
and paying rent.

The War

I lost my voice there for a while
let it curl at the corners, tattered and worn.
Misused and misplaced.
Chased metaphors which led to nowhere,
empty shells of meaning lay strewn across my floor
from bullets I had fired.
Aimed at myself
yet wounding you.
Aimed at you
yet killing myself.

Not that instant
bullet to the heart,
life falls appart,
"What the fuck am I doing?!"
kind of death...
No.
The secret kind.
The kind of death
that seeps poison into your veins
slowly
each day.

Feeding me just enough to stay alive
yet denying me of the nutrition
of truth;
until I was a hollow shell of the woman
I know I can be.
Just enough left of me

to keep walking.
Keep barking orders and insults.
Keep gritting my teeth and holding up my defences
in case anyone got in.
But not enough
for there to be anything left
to get into.

It's funny how once the people starve away,
bodies lost to war and hunger,
all that remains
are rusting tanks,
crumbling walls, and empty defence systems
with no one left to protect.

The scattered bones
of what was once
a family.

Consequences

To the ones who don't speak up.
Don't run away.
Don't leave.

To the ones who lay there every night
dealing with wandering hands
in silence.
Dealing with Smashing plates
in silence.
Dealing
In silence.

Or in muttered grumbles
under their breath,
or to the ears of listening friends,
punctuated with explanations
of how "on it" you are;
How much you've "got this".

When in truth,
it's got you.

It's got you
by the throat
telling you it's for your own good.
Because apparently,
being gripped by a jaw that doesn't bite
proves you are safe.

But when the wolf is pinning you down
with subtle acts of agression,
grinding down your voice,
your opinions,
your worth,
those teeth feel less like reassurance
and more like a threat.

To the ones who can not name their abusers
aloud
because the entanglement is too deep.
Because of finance,
or employment,
or health care,
or parents,
Or kids.

Who stay silent.
Because it's easier.
Because it's safer.
Because a gentle grinding down of the self
is easier to ignore
than the sudden rip into the void
that it takes to leave.

And because of the consequences.

The consequences.
The consequences.

To the ones who think so long
about the consequences

that silence feels worth it.

Despite knowing deep down
they may not be the only one.
Despite knowing deep down
they are right.
Despite knowing deep down
silence is the coward's option.
Despite knowing
but not deeply believing
their truth is valid, and worthy and real.

To the cowards.
The courageous cowards
who put their safety aside
because they can't speak up,
can't run away,
can't leave.
And if they do leave
they must do so
in silence,
to keep the peace.
To avoid the consequences.

The consequences.
The consequences.

That's the thing about abuse,
sometimes it's not what is actively happening
that creates control,
but the fear of what might happen.

The consequences.
The consequences.

The consequences that keep us silent,
keep us small,
keep us from naming names,
seeking help,
laying our boundaries,
rocking the boat.

To the ones who can't speak up,
can't run away,
can't leave.

I see you.

Fuck.
I see you
and I'm sorry.
I don't have any answers for you,
any escape routes
or eject buttons.
Who am I to tell you what to do?
I have my own secrets.
My own silent segments of my life
kept in patient insinuation
and swallowed opinions
out of fear of the consequences
I have been exposed to
too many times.

But I want you to know,
in a world who celebrates the ones who speak,

the #metoo's,
the court cases,
and the celebrity revealers.
In a world who platforms the ones
who spoke up,
who ran away,
who left.

I see you.
And this poem,
this poem,

this one's for you.

Martyr-Mother

I thought pregnancy
was the biggest surrender
I would ever know.
Five months of bed-bound sickness,
vomiting,
watching my world fall apart around me.
Watching my identity die;
my body wasting away
while another grew inside me.
My self wasting away
while another grew inside me.

Scrabbling to find some sense in it all,
telling myself
what I had always been told:
"The Martyrdom of Motherhood is the only way."
Then,
I thought birthing
was the deepest surrender
I would ever know.

The surges of pain which I howled through in primal throws,
the orgasmic laughter which stretched my cervix apart, and the
blissful depths of my drowning in post contraction bliss.

Then I learnt to love you
through sleep deprivation,
through screaming,
through clashes of wills.

Then
through depression,
through loneliness and isolation,
through heartbreak, lies, stress and manipulation.
We found home in each other.

So, I thought loving you as a solo mum
would be the deepest surrender I would ever know.

Then I learnt to love myself
through sleep deprivation,
through screaming,
through clashes of wills.
Then
through depression,
through the loneliness and isolation of it all,
through heartbreak, lies and manipulation.

Through learning boundaries, the hard way.

Learning forgiveness and compassion for myself
as the highest priority.

I thought self-love as a broken mother,
from a broken family,
was the deepest surrender I would ever know.
Then I watch you smile at me
and the whole world melts
in our love for a moment,
and I know how far we have come
together
is only one step
on a lifetime journey

of our growth.

That I will learn a million ways to surrender,
and a million ways to stay strong.
That you too shall learn this
from me,
from my mistakes,
from yourself,
and from your own.

That the Martyrdom of Motherhood
is a lie I was fed.
A lie that I
will not pass on
to you

For you do not need to be a martyr.
You need to be a master
of yourself,
of loving-kindness,
fierce-gentleness,
and the balance
of clear boundaries
and sublime surrender.

Crayons

Show me your colours.
All of them.
I can take it.
And if I can't
it's merely because
my own heart
is a melting pot
of crayons
in summer heat
and sometimes
the tones get muddy
under the mess of life
and I become colourblind
for a moment.

But I know
every tender tone,
every shade,
every subtle hue
of you
is golden
and each one,
only a single part
of a full spectrum
of brilliance
Hungering to be seen.

Foreign Sand

When blood pulsed
and my raging ocean pulled back
for the tidal crash
of skin on skin,
of new shores,
of unexplored lands;
the vision of your face
became the only break
between me
and my broken integrity.

But the desire to feel wanted
can pound stronger on the heart
than a thousand white horses
churning wild this sandy bed.
The desire to feel special
can override our true course
leaving us lost
to the whims of the storm.
The call of the wild
can split open rocks,
grind down stone,
create granules of our unity.
So even grasped fingers can not stop it
slipping away.

Once, we set sail by the stars
yet it was only the sirens song
which rendered our voyage
astray.

When hearts raced,
consequences were thrown to the wind
to become no more than shanties
whispering heartbreak to the stars.

My ocean crashed,
and tides changed.
I was left wet and waterlogged
crawling silently back
into your arms
with the gritty sensation
of foreign sand
beneath my tongue.

My Defences

Words slip from
my mouth,
my finger tips.

Words born from truth,
tainted with fear,
laced with poison,
sent.
Said.

How do we silence a screaming heart
when all she knows is words
and all she hungers for
is closeness?

Last night
we exploded
in a cacophony of stardust.
Where you held my body,
precious flowers in the wind.

My teeth hurt.
Almost as much
as my heart does.
My mouth uttering the phrase
"leave me alone".

What happened?

When those words left my heart
they said
"Let's leave this world for a moment.
Take shelter in the stars.
Fall into each other again.
Lover,
please come close.
I love you.
Step towards me.

I am scared."

But instead
I hear myself say
"Fuck off".
Mouthing my pain
like a cock I never really liked,
but sucked for the sake of security
because it was the only way I knew
how to survive.

I want you to tell me
I mean something
to you.

To brush aside my defences,
lean in
and remind me
that we are living a love
so ancient
it witnessed the first sparks
of atoms colliding.

That we are a direct result
of that big bang.
That we are stardust
and my fear is irrelevant
under the truthful gaze
of love.

But I don't tell you that,
do I?

Wayfarer

There is a thundering scream inside me
telling me to run away.
"We are born alone.
We die alone.
All else is avoidance of our own ultimate aloneness,
space filling.
You have known this forever
yet still
you insist
on filling.
On falling.
Still you insist on falling,
as if it changes a thing."

So much in me wants to pull away.
It's hard,
I'm squirming,
caught between reaction and rationality.

The pound of my heart,
the thunder of a frightened herd
of wild horses,
eyes gaping,
mouths foaming,
not even aware of what they are running from.
Just running
because staying risks too much.

"And if you can't run"
The scream says

"Then push.
Push
or run.
Push
Or run. "

It is deafening.

But,
There is another voice.
Whispering quietly,
so quietly I can barely hear her
Under the thunder
Of hooves.

"Don't.
Don't run.
Let go of the fear,
surrender.
Be water woman
because you are made of oceans
and oceans know no bounds.
These storms are integral
to the churning up
of the depth
of the movement
of tides.
To the sailing
into truth.
Stay your course
wayfarer.
It was already mapped
in the stars.

Stay your course
wayfarer,
because new ground
has never been found
within the safety
of a reef.

And woman, you are made of oceans.
Timeless.
You have existed for eternity
and always shall.

Water can run
as much as it wants
but eventually it will get hot
and rise up to the sky
and return back to the mountain
only to have to do it all again
anyway.
Running doesn't help.

Be water woman
because you are made of oceans
and no one wants to face a tidal wave.
They want waves they can contain.
Waves they can surf.
Waves they can predict.
Only the courageous
dare take on
open water.
Only the courageous
find new worlds,

get the beauty
of the true expanse
of the everythingness
and the nothingness
of your stillest days.

The sparkle on your water.

Because they see
that it is your force
which makes you powerful.
That your storms
do not take away
only add
to your splendour.

Be water woman.

And if they are ready
to navigate your storms
they shall.

Do not run.
Be the storm.
Be the gentle lapping.
Be the depth.
Be the shallows.
Be it all,
and let go.

Let go
woman
let go.

Choose You

When every cell in my body
breaks its husky shell,
cracks open its hostile defences;
when every cell
in this beautifully wounded form
chooses you

you will know.

By the way my body moves
towards your touch,
moulds
to your mouth,
surrenders to your kisses.

You will know

By the way my poetry,
written to God,
feels like it was penned
directly into your heart.

By the way I find God
in your heart.

When every cell in my body
chooses you
you will know
by the look of fear in my eyes.

It's not romantic to say it
but it's true,
when I choose you
shit will come up.
Wild torrents of self-sabotage,
self-judgements,
self-deprecation.
Wild torrents of
feelings.

So many feelings.

But when I choose you
you will know

Because my fear will be handed to you
gently
in a whisper of
"These are the parts of me
I am petrified to see.
Look at them
with me.
Please."

It's so easy to love a poet
for her ferocity,
for her passion,
for her capacity to speak her way
through her pain.

It's so easy to love a poet
on the stage.

Where the mess is kept in paragraphs
and metaphors,
tidied into stanzas.
Where hyperbole feels poetic,
not melodramatic.
and when she speaks the final word,
steps away from the microphone,
the feelings are left there
hovering
cathartically
under the lights.

They do not make it into the car,
into the drive home.
They do not make it into the bed,
into your arms.
They do not get cried out upon your skin,
or behind your back.

It's so easy to love a poet
on the stage.

But when I choose you
my poetry is uncontained.
It spills off the page.
Wraps its way through my teeth,
slips out when we make love
and war.
Slips out when we make dinner
and more,
when I feel starved
or satiated.

When every cell
in this beautifully wounded form
chooses you,
there is no leaving the poetry,
the feelings,
on the stage.

They weave their way
into every moment.

It's fucking intense.
And I love it.
And I'm petrified of it.
And I love it.
And I'm petrified of you.
And I love you.

So I ask you;
can you see the poetic credit
in the melodrama?
Can you see the truth
in my metaphors?
Can you read the unspoken moments
in our communication
with as much trust
of my skills
as the silent pauses
I suspend you in
amongst an audience
of strangers?

Can you love me

in my fierceness
and in my fears?
In my passion
and in my pain?

Can you love every refrain,
every syllable,
every pregnant pause
of my form?

Because when every cell
in my body
chooses you,
it will be wild,
and raw,
and real.
It will be filled
with the most profound
truth,
and love,
and pain,
and light,
and darkness
you have ever tasted.

My body will move
towards your touch,
melt
to your mouth,
write poetry
onto your heart;
and there is no turning back.

The Hard Road

If I could do it again
I'm not sure I would know any other way.
It has always been my nature
to forge down a path half beaten,
half wild.
To leave myself half stranded,
half held.
To ostracise myself
from those I love.
To be in the arms
of strangers.
To find strength in the battle
of discomfort
over ease.
Yet here I am
searching for soft pillows and skins
because once again
I chose the hard road.
The one which meant
I didn't
run
away.

A Translation

When I say
"I don't trust that you love me for who I am",
what I am telling you is
"I have been told my whole life that I can not be loved simply for
my self".

When I say
"the other woman is more beautiful/inspiring/sexy/fun",
what I am letting you know is
"I have been taught my whole life to compare myself to my
sisters, so there are times that I no longer really know what's true,
and it destroys me from the inside out."

When I say
"I don't think my opinion/feeling/experience is worth speaking"
What I am telling you is
"I have been told my whole life to be silent. Quiet. Small.
I have been interrupted, told I don't know what I am talking
about, denied opportunities purely on the credentials of my
gender.
I have been told over and over again that what I feel and
experience is not truth but the wildness of a woman's landscape.
I have been told I could be institutionalised for those things.
I have grown up to the sounds of women's nails on concrete walls
searching for a way out of their own emotions,
for an escape from who they are,
for a gateway back into acceptance"

When I am saying
"I'm too fat/skinny/tall/short."

what I am telling you is
"I can not trust I am safe to be seen.
That I have been told I do not fit.
It is so ingrained now that I do not always know the extent of my
power."

When I say "I can't wear that because I'll look like a slut"
What I'm letting you know is,
my whole life my worth had been reduced to how I look.
What I'm saying is
that my sexuality has been stolen and sold back to me again with
harsh guidelines.
That my sexuality is not mine to own
but other's to put upon me.
That I must be consumable in the most palatable way,
else I risk judging eyes, whispered comment, groping hands, rape,
death.

When I am saying
"I struggle to hear you when you say that you love me"
What I am telling you is that I have been told not to love myself
from the earliest months of my life.
I have been told that love is conditional
and I am in no condition to receive it.

What I am saying is
I am unpacking all this bullshit.
I am a battlefield of scars trying desperately to grow poppies.
That I function,
and I function really well.
But, there are times when I have to sift through and counteract
a lifetime of statements made about me
before I can find the truth.

86

That I am still finding the truth.

That I'm still unpacking this
every moment of every day.

So,
when you sit there;
hear me say all this.

When I am wild, raw, crying.
When I am closed, shy, small.
When I am not in my most shining self,
yet still you bask in my glow

When instead of hearing
"You are failing me"
you hear
"society has failed me and I can not help but project that on to
you right now".

When you hear me
and in response
you tell me you love me;
you tell me over and over again,
uttering my light,
fueling my worth,
reimprinting my self back onto myself,

and then you walk away without judging me
for being emotional, hysterical, slutty, bitchy.

You walk away carrying that compassionate incandescent
image of me in your heart.

You
are unpacking
hundreds of years
of systematic silencing,
of cultural shaming,
of patriarchal wounding,
mansplaining,
sexism,
misogyny,
abuse,
with me.

Thank you.

Meniscus

- The Eros & The Amor -

I, like many women, have had sex and love stolen from me, ripped from my being. I have been slut-shamed, queer-shamed, love-shamed. I have been told I am not worthy of love. Not worthy of sex.
Then.
I have been sold sex and love. Packaged into vanilla sex, and "Boy-meets-girl, happy-ever-after" Disney love stories.
Sex is in slow-mo, with a down beat soundtrack and pert nipples.
There is no mess, no clumsy ripping off of clothes, no stopping for water breaks, no need for lube, or giggling at pussy farts.

But when I fall in love, it is deep and messy, full of nuance, and not bound by gender. When I swim in eros, it is dirty, and powerful, and emotive, and full of flavour. There is kink and there is tenderness.
It swells into a meniscus of emotion and sensation, until I am so full all I can do is kiss, and fuck and write poetry.

This is mine.

"I refuse to live in the ordinary world as ordinary women. To enter ordinary relationships. I want ecstasy."
| Anaïs Nin, The Diary of Anaïs Nin, Vol 1 1931–1934 |

Fear

When love looks like this
it lifts the heavy head
of fear,
looks deep into its eyes
and says
"Yes. I see you.
Yes. You are welcome here."

Fear is not the enemy,
it is the sound of rusty hinges
as your doors
begin
to open.

Adrift

I've been dreaming of you for such a long time
that this reality seems strange.
It's like my body can't accept that you're on my lips,
not on the page.
I keep catching myself trying to convince me it's not true.
Your blue eyes a mirage
a figment of my mind.
Part of me is still gripping to the shorelines
because a fantasy
doesn't make
a safe ship
to sail,
even on the smoothest sea.

And I've been dreaming of you
for such a long time,
that I'm
not sure you're actually real.
So I find that I'm
already preparing for the day
that the mirage fades
and I'm left stranded
in a desert I built myself.
Where every grain of sand
is another one of my fantasies
that I have ground down
by rubbing it against the truth.
By rubbing it against you.

How unfair that is.

But I have been dreaming of you
for such a long time
that I don't think I can bear
not to take that risk.
Your kiss
just another reason
to make you real.
The way your lips tease me
into you.
The way
you are as soft
as I had imagined.
The way I can hear the ocean
when I utter your name.

And you see
when I pinch myself
It actually hurts,
and every time I wake up
there's a message from you
on my phone,
and I don't know how much longer
I can keep telling myself this isn't true.
Because
Soon
I will slip.
Let my self adrift,
and dive deeply
in
to you.

Beautiful Hands

She told me
I have beautiful hands.
Not your average compliment
I must admit
but not one I am unfamiliar with;
It's one I have been handed
many times in my life.

You see,
my fingers seem to draw attention,
hold the gaze.
The way they finger that line
between slender
yet strong.
The way delicacy dances
with dexterity.
The way thread passes
through needle
with ease.
Yarn tangles
around hook
with speed.
Wool spins
into strands,
wood weaves
into baskets,
strings meet
and release

into rhythms
and beats.

How skin pricks up
into a thousand swollen hills,
folds open,
damp with expectation.
Her mouth
agape.
A gasp.
A grasping moment.
A tender caress.
Her back arched
beneath me,
she swells
into a thousand
dying stars,
a thousand rivers
meeting,
a thousand breaths
into one.

She told me
I have beautiful hands,
so
I held her.

Static In The Mist

It's madness
how we can't seem
to get close
enough.

No matter how deep
you go,
how firm
I hold you,
how much
you kiss
my mouth,

my cells still hunger
for you
to slip your way
into the spaces between them;
so our very particles
may know
the ecstacy
of this dance.

What is it?
To merge so fully
wth another human
that love itself becomes atomic
and we are only
static in the mist.

Hoddle Street

I'm on my way to work,
navigating the throb of traffic
through the moaning of rain
and I'm hit with it.

Like a nostalgic smell,
one that winds its way through my soul,
consuming my heart.
Suddenly,
it's you.

My body aches
for you.
Testing my capacity
to fantasise
and drive
at the same time,

Hoddle Street
has never been more
thrilling
than right in this moment.
With the bubbling sensation
of your phantom lips
on the nape
of my neck,
leaving
my body
wet,

my mind
a mess,
my heart
hungry
for
you.

How can a stranger feel so familar?

Perhaps it's just timing, or science, or something about it being a
"Scorpio Moon"...perhaps it's love, or hyperbole, or the addiction
to dopamine in our brains...

But the touch of your fingers
on my body
feels more like home
than the brick and mortar in which I reside.
It's as if
I were touching myself.
Holding myself

As in, you touch me
how I touch me
in my mind.

As in, you are now in my mind
touching me
how you touch me
In reality;

and isn't that a thing?
When fantasy and reality align,

when we dream it real,
and the world and our mind
harmonise
to create
this.

This feeling.

This feeling.

What a gift
it is.

So thank you.

Softness

I lost myself
for a moment
in the softness
of you.

Northern Rain

I fell asleep to the sounds
of northern rain pounding on the roof,
and awoke this morning
to thoughts
of what I didn't do.
The air could feel it.
Electricity.
The crack of sky and earth not quite meeting,
the space between my top lip
and my bottom lip,
and the thing I didn't say,
or the thing I didn't do.

My lips conduits for a storm,
as if lightning bolts
were lighting up the space between us
and we,
separated by science,
remained distant.
Because, if the sky and earth collided
wouldn't that be madness?
Wouldn't that be what gods had battled against
for millennia?
Wouldn't that be wild?
If sky and earth collided,
wouldn't that be a risk?

and what is a storm
if not a risk?

I always thought lightning came from the sky.
A build up of energy
which can not contain itself
so it strikes
to find peace
in the stillness of the earth.

But then, I was told that wasn't true.
That actually it is me,
I mean, the earth,
which lets it loose.
The charge within this mass of earth and stone
lets loose to the sky.

Either way,
feels like a risk right?

A one way charge,
it feels like a risk.

So there's things we don't do,
despite the sparks.
Things we keep distant,
separated by science.
Because, if the earth and sky colided,
wouldn't that be madness?

So I did, what any earth would do,
I woke up,
and I Googled it.
"Does lightning go up or down?"
I asked.

The answer, as is often the way,
is both.
For lightning to occur the sky must be so full of passion,
So full it breaks its own rules,
extends its hands
down,
low enough
so the earth can feel it.
At this point, it seems,
the earth raises herself,
her lips alive with desire,
and, following the path laid out by the clouds,
she extends herself
up.
Their charge
ever stronger
when combined.

And it is here,
the storm
becomes alive.

A crack of light.
A spark of passion which reverberates across the night,
making the hair of mortal souls
stand up on end.
Because, when the sky and earth colide,
it's wild.
And there's something eternally intriguing
about the savage nature
of chemistry
and biology,

about bodies,
and souls,
and kissing.

About storms.

As I write this
the sun is pretending
nothing happened.
Trying to write a different story.
A new day story,
with the innocent song
of dawn chorus,
and breakfast.

However,
I can hear
the gentle drops
of midnight rain
falling from the leaves
outside,
and I remember
a storm took place.
Even if a kiss
didn't.

Fold In

Haven't we always been?
As in,
there is an indefinite quality
to the way our bodies
fold in
to one another.

As if,
we are fitting back into shapes
our souls have made
a million
times before.

As in,
any rising doubts that I feel
are instantly soothed
the moment
you touch me.

As if,
you have always been touching me
and somehow we
didn't realise
until this moment.

As in,
this moment is eternal
as now we continuously
sink into
each other again.

Ropes

You cannot fake this
bliss.
The moment the last rope falls
away,
the stillness begins.

"Why do you do it?" People ask.
As if it's about the ropes.
As if it's about the restraint.
As if it's about feeling the oppression.
As if I'm a stranger to oppression.
As if I'm unaware of the power play
of a man tying me down,
stringing me up,
binding my desires.

I am not ignorant
to these facts.

To the devastating mirror
I look into
every time I submit,
or surrender.

So, why do I do it?

Because you cannot fake this
bliss.
The moment the last rope falls

away,
the stillness that is found
in that moment.
In the unbinding.
In the holding.
In the knowing,
once again,
you were taken to your edge.
But this time
you were brought back
safe.

Blindfolded

Blindfolded,
we fumble for peace.
Your skin, a holy altar
I had bowed down to
moments before.
The salt stains on my cheeks
fading.
Bathed in
sweat,
blood,
cum.

What kind of prayer is this?

Obedience

My body will not sit,
obedience has abandoned me,
I am wild
with desire.

You have awoken something in me.

And it keeps me wanting,
keeps me writhing,
keeps me running over the vision
of your smiling eyes
in my mind.
Over and over again,
until I am swimming
in my own pleasure.
Drowning
in my own desire.

How have you done this to me?

Taken all rational thoughts
and replaced them with your face.
So even now,
after days in your embrace,
when I am alone
with the beauty of space
around me,
with time to think,
and create,
and dance.

All I can do
is picture your eyes
peeking over the rim
of your sun glasses.
Looking at me like that.
Looking at me
like love
looks into the face of fear.
Looking at me
in the way the bee
regards the flower.
In the way the flower
regards the sun.
In the way the sun
Regards the moon,
casting his radiance out
so she becomes vibrant
even in the darkness.
Basking.
Basking.
Basking.

Even when I am alone,
or with another,
somehow I am still basking
in you.

My body will not sit.
Obedience has abandoned me.
I am wild
with desire
for you.

Tectonic

We have the tremendous force
of tectonic plates.
We are worlds colliding.
This, my love,
is how mountains are made.

Ripples

I am still rippling
outwards
from the descent
of your touch,
As you dove into me.
As we
dove into
each other.
Hours swimming
in skin and the sound
that is made
when string and bow
sing together.
A melody so raw
I could not
let go
without letting go.
My body singing out
a haunting refrain,
a shanty's lilt
of longing.
We crash together,
never quite,
but almost,
but not.
Over
and over.
Skin,
and ocean,

and lips,
and waves.
My body ripples now.
Days past,
and still I cannot clean
the feeling
of ocean spray from my thighs.
I am hungry
and satiated,
simultaneously.
Rippling outwards,
alone
in my bed.
Sailing on a memory
of you.

Furious Love

The taste of your breath
leaves me wanting
to devour
every inch of you.

Perhaps this should have been a warning sign,
because no one wants to be swallowed whole.
It's a fact I've discovered,
over time.

So I take you in,
in tiny morsels.
Shit you out again
in poetry,
and song

Nibbling at your edges.
Because no one wants to be consumed
by a love
as furious
as this.

Not Just Sex

And I don't know
if it's ok to admit this.
It's
not just sex for me.
Not quite love,
but,
you see,
a seed
has planted.
Has taken root.
And now my soul
has sewn a hole
shaped for a piece of you.

Her

Your body ripples
under my fingertips.
Your lip curled,
your body arched back,
my mind captivated
in the way the shadows
map the contours of your
skin.
My hand placed
in the space between your breasts.
My other
placed
in the space
between your legs.
Your body ripples
beneath my fingertips,
and I am captivated
by your every breath.

Cocoon

Every time
I leave
the cocoon
of your embrace,
I am changed.

A Night In The Swag

The morning laid its stillness down upon us
like a blanket of gentle rain,
silencing all but the birds
and the beat of our hearts.

It is here I find myself
content.
Our bodies gently leaning into one another.
Your arms,
vine-like around my form.
My heart,
swollen from the thousands of ways
we pray together.

Silence The Ocean

My body wrenches itself
upwards.
Curves its way through space and time,
to find a breath,
to find a moment,
to find some kind of peace
amongst this wildness.

Your arms are the safest place I know.

I know
I've said it to you
a million times
already,
and still it does not yet
feel said.
So, I fumble around
with words,
and chords,
and ink on broken pages,
trying to find a better way to express
this noise
in my heart.

But how do you silence the ocean?

You can't.
Even in its stillest moments
it still sings.

And I have not known silence
since the first night
you laid your hands
upon my body.

Only songs,
and words,
and moans of pleasure,
and the wild cacophony of my soul
cracking open
further,
and further.

The sound of walls crumbling.
The sound of two hearts
finding each other again,
after an eternity appart.
In fresh bodies.
As if the life before was not enough
to quench their thirst,
to stop the tides,
to not inevitably find themselves
inexplicably entwined
in each others lives,
once again.

Our lips crash together,
the oceans part,
and I am soaked through
filled with you;
So when I close my eyes
I am only static

in the mist.

How do you silence the ocean?

I can not.
I can only find a million ways
to sing along.

Howling To The Wind

- The Grieving -

What can we do in those moments, when the
whole world disappears from beneath our feet?
In grief? In despair? In bitter-sweet longing and pain?

You cannot run from grief.
It knows you, follows you, hunts you down; and once you
think you are free, it crawls out of the shadows and sinks
itself deep into your chest.

We cannot run from our grief as we can not run from our
reflection.

I'll see you there.

"How do I hold faith with sun in a sunless place?"
| Audre Lourde, A Burst of Light: and Other Essays |

Coffee

She held her cup.
I held my breath.
The silence became a bitterness
we could no longer drink.

Change

There is a change in the air,
a hint of something on the horizon,
a smell on the wind
which blows in cold now
from the south.
I pull my hood up
and keep walking.

I used to be afraid of change,
and at times, I guess I still am.

Afraid of where it may take me,
or leave me.
Shattered and wind whipped.
Alone.
But what are we
if not alone?

Lying to ourselves I guess.

But today, the feel of my scarf
wrapped around my neck
reminds me that some changes
take away
only to make space
for what else may come.

The fire of summer
has left me

ready
for winter flames.

The green
has left us
lamenting the fall
of leaves.

Poetry. Even here.

Her love left me
hollow.
A cavern ready
to be filled.

I pull my hood up
and keep walking.

Massacre

Bits of you
lay strewn across my house,
extended limbs of love
severed.
I bag up
this massacre
and hope
no evidence
remains.

After She Left

She was sad I only talked
about my heartbreak
when I referred to her.

As if this was an insult.

As if "heartbreak"
wasn't enough
to allude to the depth
of aching and joy
and oneness
I felt in our love.

As if "heartbreak"
was a light pebble
thrown into the shallow pool
of my poetry,
and not a volcano
erupting from the depth of my soul.
Screaming to the world,
not only of the anguish of loss,
but the beauty of having
been in it in the first place.

As if "Heartbreak" was the cause,
and not the symptom,
of having unfurled myself
so inexplicably open,
that the juicy

gaping
mouth
of my heart
is now left
to the elements
of the dry
harshness
of grief.

She was sad I only talk about
my heartbreak
when referring to her,
instead of the profound depth
of what it feels like
to have someone see you
completely,
and love what they see.
Or her smile.
The lines around her eyes.
How my body tremors under her gaze.
Her touch.
How laughing with her
was like laughing with myself
except finally
I wasn't
alone.

She was sad I only talked about
my heartbreak
when referring to her,
as if she had left me
with anything else.

Heartbreak & Dating Apps

Heartbroken
I search
desperately
for someone to hug,
or someone to fuck.
Someone to distract me
from this pain.

Dating apps don't work the way
I imagined they would.

I cannot laser beam in
some other aching heart,
so we can wrap ourselves around
each other
and weep into each other's
sacred places;
muffling the howls of our despair
into each others orgasmic screams,
like I wish I could.

Partly, because
science doesn't work like that yet
and partly, because
whatever heart came to me
it wouldn't be
Hers.

I Want Who I Should Not

The darkness of midnight
cannot bind bodies that hunger.

For she is a blanket we hide beneath
from the ever-present cold.

More, it is the light of day,
the harsh glare of perspective,

which may make us want
to close our eyes.

8 Years Of Autumn

There is a line of trees
(London plane, I think,
but my memory could be wrong)
that edge a park
in Brighton town.

I would walk beneath them
every day,
kicking leaves
as I went.

The crisp air
brittle
with salt
and the promise
of winter
approaching.

They spoke to me
once.
"Touch me"
they said.
But I never did.
Eight years
and I never did.

Eight years
of Autumn.
He still haunts

a room
in the corner
of my heart.

"Touch me"
I whisper.
Sending out
the occasional email
to a long dead address
to a long lost
love.

Like dropping acorns
down
into vast catacombs
in the hope
an oak tree
may grow.

In the hope
he may reply.

An acknowledgement
of the seasons
we shared
or something.
Something.

Now those trees
turn crisp once more,
but neither of us
walk beneath them

kicking up storms
of last season's stories.
Neither of us
rush drunken
through the dark cold streets
of Brighton,
hoping to collapse
eventually
in each other's arms.

But the London Planes
still stand
shedding skin,
and leaves,
and stories of past seasons.
And I still stand
shedding skins,
and leaves,
and stories of our seasons.

And he
still stands
somewhere
sweeping acorns off his floor.

Grief

Grief is a dangerous beast.
It crawls its way beneath your skin,
takes hibernation in your guts,
and raises its head
in the most unexpected places.

So I hold you tenderly.
Mute my hunger
to wrap myself around you,
consume your being within me.
Hold of these strangely
maternal,
yet sexual
desires
to soothe you
and fuck you.
To soothe you
by fucking you.
To soothe your pain
by immersing you
in the endless depths
of my body
and love.

Because I know,
when grief takes control of my heart
all I want
is to escape into selfish
bliss.

To melt into flesh.
To feel less alone.
Or to be taken to those places
where I cannot hide
from what I feel
because all I have become
is feeling,
and silence,
and noise.

But you,
you are different,
and I am not here to soothe myself.
So, I quieten my desires
and gently wrap my arms
around your tired form.
Let you fluster.
Let you cry.
Let you distract yourself
with cleaning, or movies, or food.

Gently wrap my arms
around your tired form,
and hold you until
you sleep.

Ships

There is a potent stillness
in the space between us.
The moment before
two atoms collide;
where push and pull
are of equal force.
Where right and wrong
are both valid concepts.
Where your head
Is resting
against mine,
your fingers
brushing against mine,
and I can taste you
in the air around me.

But we are like ships
and this is our night.
And I'd like to say we must have patience,
but patience is still
loaded with the presumption
that we will eventually land
on the same beach
at the same time.

And I have learnt the hard way
not to wait on beaches,
not to hold my heart out
for a boat which may never come.

So for now we sit,
moments apart,
silently hungering
for impact.

I drink you in
from a distance.
Taste you in the air around us.
Revel in
the poignant pause
where we could collide
but don't.

And silently smile
as you walk away,
warm with the knowing
that once again
we crossed courses
in the night.

Canyons

I remember wanting you so badly
my body would tremble
at a picture of your face.

Once I had to sit down, drink water;
clear the dizzying heights of my hunger.

You said it was the same for you,
but truth doesn't always live itself
and I felt your absence in our quiet moments.

There were always reasons.
Reasons not to touch.
Reasons not to love.
Reasons not to surrender.

One day I walked to the beach
leaving you alone
in bed.
I was wild with wanting.
You were on the other side of a canyon
looking at me
with those blue eyes
I had fallen in love with
silently.

My body trembled
so I walked away,
not wanting to impose my love

where it was not wanted.

So I took myself to the shoreline,
the sand slipping between my toes.

So I stripped my clothes.
Let myself be taken,
angry fucking the waves.
I let her pound me,
sweep me off my feet.
She crashed across my chest,
I left
breathless
with every swell
of her.
I left
selfless
with every kiss
of her.
I left
softened,
until air left my body,
body left my pain.
Until I was bliss soaked through,
wet,
drenched,
wishing it had been you
all along.

Like a rebound fuck
you know you needed,
but you wished you hadn't,

because her skin
was never quite the right
woman.

When I returned
I told you where I had been
and why.
You made some playful comment
to hide your own hurt.
Sipped your coffee.
Walked away
across a canyon
I had never known how to cross.

You became a metaphor
tied into my poetry,
a memory
of oceans
that promised a depth
they never revealed.

Ending Gently

So if it is
that we are falling apart,
let us do it
with love.

So, as we crumble,
the dust of us
settles
a tender
amorous ash
of acceptance
across this
earth.

And So It Is...
- The Remembering -

I forget, so often, I forget;
so, I must be reminded.

I am woman, yes.
I am fierce, yes.
I am grief, and loss, and hunger, yes.
I am passion, and sex, and love.

And I am tears, so many tears.

But at the end of the day, I am just another spirit in
a bag of meat and matter,
tired from all this human work,
longing to go home.

*"I was born when all I once
feared - I could
love"*
| Rabia of Basra |

The Weight

Why do I put God onto you?
As if that is something
you could carry;
the weight of those expectations,
the weight of my devotion.

Why do I take God out of you?
As if that Is something
you could not carry;
the weight of those expectations ,
the weight of my devotion.

Reminders

"What is it to love?"
She said to the rain

The rain kissed her face,
and fell away again.
Kissed her face,
and fell away again

Seeping into her flesh
yet never diverting
from its path.

What is this devotion?
Where two bodies merge,
yet, do not lose themselves
in each other?

In The Arms Of A Man

I am sorry
Beloved,
I had forgotten
you could exist
in the arms
of a man.
In the grip
of a man.
In the heart
of a man.

So one night
you came to
remind me.

Touched me
through his fingers.
Kissed me
through his lips.
Held me
so gently,
yet so firmly,
in his arms.

It was all I could do,
not to fall into you
so deeply
that even breath
would seem

irrelevant.

But I had to.

I had to breathe;
So as not to lose focus
with his eyes.
His incredible eyes.
So as not to lose sight
of you there
again.

Jasmine

I wish
I were made of
jasmine,
so all I needed to do
was exist,
be inhaled,
and life became complete
for a moment.

So that my
blossoming
was regulated,
clockwork,
consistent.

So that my own
heady scent
could envelop my aching heart
and bring peace
to these
twilight moments.

Irrelevant

The dissolving of self
into another's tender flesh
can be a substance we crave
like heroine,
or psylocybin,
or love.

Because, sometimes we need
to be reminded
we are golden,
yet simultaneously
irrelevant,
in the eyes
of God.

Humancentric

"We are so afraid
of being alone"
I said to the morning.

The morning sat
and listened.
The sunlight kissed my skin,
a bird landed on a nearby branch,
chirruped a song
I had not heard before,
and as the wind sighed
a small white butterfly
penetrated my periphery.

The morning,
she took a breath,
looked at me and said:
"How very humancentric of you
my love"

Gratitude

Massive gratitude to all my Patreon supporters and my
Kickstarter supporters who financially supported me to create
this book; I can not explain how encouraging that is.

Deep loving gratitude to my lovers, family, and friends who have
filled me so greatly they have re-emerged into my poetry, you
know who you are, and to those of you who have challenged me
so fully that art has been born.

Special shout outs:
Kaia for your profound love and inspiration, I'm so proud of you.
My parents, all of you, for your never ending support, I miss you.
Rory, for reminding me of what it means to be safe, and loving
me so unconditionally.

Mel, for being the sounding board for my darknss so often, the
epic sister I've needed in my life and incredible not-wife and
second mama for my girl.

I love you all so deeply.

Also, Maggi and Dom for proofreading and not judging me
harshly for my grammar and punctuation sins.
Massive gratitude to Broken Isn't Bad for capturing my words in
beautiful illustrations.

Thank you, you beautiful humans.

About The Author.

Originally from the UK, Fleassy Malay studied at The BRIT School of Performance Art in London, and at Brighton University. Since then she has moved to Australia and performed across 4 continents building a global following.

As a queer artist, writer and single mum to her red-head, 5-year old daughter, the line between work, art, and life is very thin for Fleassy Malay.

Her work took a leap in 2018 when her poem, Witches, was released by Uplift Connect and swiftly soared to over 3 million views. This was followed by two TEDx talks in 2019 and the release of her album, Unhear This.

With a fierce passion for women's rights and LGBTQI+ visibility, she has never been one to shy away from adversity and taboo topics.

In 2012 she founded "Mother Tongue - Women Speak", a Melbourne based organisation focused on platforming women's voices. She went on to coach speaking, confidence, and presence through courses, trainings, and private sessions.
She now educates internationally on the power of reclaiming our courageous voices. She also runs her online group mentorship program, Rise - Speaker Training.

Printed in Australia
AUHW011630050820
331742AU00004B/4